I0145555

This Way to the Acorns

ALSO BY THE AUTHOR

·

POETRY

How to Kill Poetry

Road Work Ahead

Mute

St. Michael's Fall

FICTION

Men with Their Hands: A Novel

PROSE

Notes of a Deaf Gay Writer: 20 Years Later

Whispers of a Savage Sort and Other Plays
about the Deaf American Experience

Assembly Required: Notes from a Deaf Gay Life

Snooty: A Comedy

Silence Is a Four-Letter Word: On Art & Deafness

AS EDITOR

Eyes of Desire 2: A Deaf GLBT Reader

When I Am Dead: The Writings of George M. Teegarden

Eyes of Desire: A Deaf Gay & Lesbian Reader

www.raymondluczak.com

This Way to the Acorns: Poems

The Tenth Anniversary Edition

Raymond Luczak

Handtype Press
Minneapolis

Acknowledgments

"One Indian Summer" originally appeared as "One Indian Summer, Long Ago" in *The Tactile Mind*.

"Mrs. Kichak's Plum Tree" first appeared in Jill Jepson's *No Walls of Stone: An Anthology of Deaf and Hard of Hearing Writers* (Gallaudet University Press).

Special thanks go to the following people who've enabled the 2002 edition of this book to happen in some form or other: Adrean Clark, Ronnie Cohen, Marilyn Hacker, Mario Hernandez, Ned O'Gorman, James Thomas Sharer *(in memoriam)*, Tom Steele, Robin Taylor, Phillip Ward, and every reader who'd wondered if there was more after *St. Michael's Fall*. In 2012, I must thank Bryan Borland, Tom Bull, David Cummer, John Stutte, and Pia Taavila.

Most of all, I owe an eternally huge cornucopia of thanks to John Lee Clark.

Copyright Notice

This Way to the Acorns: Poems (The Tenth Anniversary Edition). Copyright © 2012 by Raymond Luczak.

Cover art: "Belly of Winter" by Robin Taylor. Copyright © 2002 by Robin Taylor.

Photograph by Raymond Luczak. Copyright © 2012 by Raymond Luczak.

Cover design by Mona Z. Kraculdy.

This book was originally published by The Tactile Mind Press in July 2002. This edition adds a new afterword by the author.

All rights reserved. No part of this book can be reproduced in any form by any means without written permission from the publisher. Please address inquiries to:

Handtype Press, LLC
PO Box 3941
Minneapolis, MN 55403-0941
USA

www.handtype.com

Printed in the United States of America.
ISBN: 978-0-9798816-2-6
Third Edition

for my siblings —

Jean Marie

Carole Ann

Mark Edward

David John

Joseph Gerard

Mary Edwardine

Andra Lee

Kevin Francis

&

all their children

WINTER

SPRING

SUMMER

AUTUMN

WINTER

ACORNS I

At Spruce and Oak Streets
they are sleeping.
Their knit caps have been pulled
snugly over their ears.
Their cheeks are a rose brown,
frozen numb under inches and
inches of calming snow.
But then they feel the
sudden pressure
of a boy's snowmobile boots
across the layers above.
They awake, alarmed,
but remember that in spring
the garrulous soil will weaken,
adopt them as their own.
They dream of sprouting green,
taking a firmer stance
against the tiring seasons.

THE FIRST SNOW

I woke up and found the sudden snow:
a white fur lining to everything
in the backyard, the sideyard, the front. *Snow*,
I shouted. *We got our first snow!*
I ate my Cream of Wheat, and dried my hands
before I struggled to tuck my navy blue snow-
suit into boots. We waddled out on the snow,
crisscrossing the sidewalks and looking behind
for the crumbs of snow falling off behind
our feet. Patches of wet gleamed in the snow-
covered sidewalks. Andra stood in the sideyard
and yelled, *How come no snowman in the sideyard?*

We scrambled all over to the sideyard
and began. I scooped up a sludge of snow
with my mittens, and rolled it through the sideyard
to make it even bigger. The white sideyard
was a blanket of lint, latching onto everything
it came in touch with. The sideyard's
brown grasses underneath made the sideyard
a tattered banner to summers gone past. My hands
smoothed the rough clumps of my ball flat; my hands
felt hot inside my mittens. Toward the sideyard's
center David and Joe pushed behind
their huge ball, now the snowman's fat behind.

Mary brushed off lintballs of grasses off its behind
while Jean waved Carole to come across the sideyard.
We all looked up when Mom waved to us behind
the kitchen window, and continued pushing behind
Jean and Carole's oval ball of snow,
and it took, finally, four of us to pull it behind
the snowman. Mark, David, and Joe laughed at its behind
and boobs until Carole hacked off those things.

(It did seem, though, she'd ruined everything
until Mark pushed his knee in to make a cleft in the behind.)
I rolled my ball a bit more, and lifted with my hands
to see how heavy it was. I waved Kevin over with my hands.

He carried his tiny ball, and with my hands
I smashed it flat all over my ball. Mary—from behind
the snowman—pointed to us with her hand
and said, *Look! We got a head now!* With my hands
I heaved it up to my waist. The sideyard's
center seemed a long distance, what with my hands
buckling under the weight, almost slipping under my hands.
As I tried to roll it up higher, the snow
fell apart like dry cookie batter. Jean said, *Oh,
we can still use it*, and pushed with her hands
the broken chunks together. *Now we got everything.*
Then David said, *A snowman's not everything*

if he can't smile. So looking under everything
where the snow had covered, we found with our hands
nine pebbles, one tooth for each of us. Everything
looked done until Andra said, *He don't have everything.
Where's his hat?* I ran into the house, the door behind
me banging shut. I yelled, *Mom! You have anything
he can wear?* I flew out with a hunter's cap—that thing
now stood out in the white grayness of the sideyard.
The snowman smiled under his brim-halo in the sideyard.
Mark tromped back across the street and said, *One more thing.*
He stuck two branches into the middle ball. *Now the snow-
man's got arms.* We felt the gentle flakes of snow

resting anew on our shoulders. Joe threw a snow-
ball over Andra's head and hit smack on Jean's behind.
Before we knew it, everyone and everything
were assaulted with a blitzkrieg from all our hands.
The snowman stood steady in the sideyard.

THE DOE

Her tail the last of her tattered tutu,

shaky white speckles against brown,

her awkward round eyes,

a constantly thawing nose,

and a shivery breath:

In my mitt is a rotting apple,

a summer having gone too fast.

Her legs, long and slender

like a gawky ballerina's,

stumble on pointe toes

on the thin sheen of white.

I lay the apple before her

and step backwards as she sails

through the air to her ravenous finish.

Her eyes never leave mine.

I too am hungry for more.

FROM THE KITCHEN WINDOW

What had been old and gray is white
at noon. It hurts my eyes to see.
Mrs. Kichak's apple tree loses more bark,
black confetti atop white dunes.
Cars crawl up the street
with brown snot around their tires.
I touch the window with a warm fingertip.

The icicles are curtains ragged from the cold.
They hang heavily and drip in the sun
at noon. A rotting apple falls,
breaks the thin eggshell of ice for the snow.
Tonight rabbits will zigzag nearby
before the apple disappears.
Their footprints will freeze before dawn.

Gasps of loose snow scatter suddenly
from the roof above. The icicles are
covered, lemonade powder on wet fingers.
I squint at a long branch
sagging from a thick white boa.
It cracks, falls. It rolls over,
free now to go anywhere.

THE MOUSETRAP
for Ronald L. Coffey 1960 - 1994

One night I found him dead, his head
a sore thumb under the vise
behind the freezer. His fur was
a cloak darker than cobwebs
hanging flies like ornaments.
I whispered, *Hello?* to the cold
drafts as I peered against the warm
hum of the freezer. I snapped
my fingers, but still: Nothing.
The December chill crept past
my long underwear as I wrestled
with a heavy hoe to bring the dirt-
scattered edge of his trap
closer. His smell overwhelmed me: How
could a thing so small be so strong?
On the cement floor, he remained
grim under the glaring light bulb.
I stared away at his vacant eyes,
a thousand dull silences
demanding an answer for this.

ANGELS

Arms as wide as heaven under the skies and
     boots atop the ridge of snowbanks, I let
go my balance. Sheets of snowflakes shook dust on
     neck, wrists; I shivered
from sudden dabs on my neck, already melted.
     Opening my eyes to the skies, I saw the
clouds billow in gray. As I flapped my arms past
     head to waist, I felt
fluttery flakes poof away for those wings of
     mine. I opened my legs like a pair of scissors,
magnificent folds of my gown. My mind dreamed
     skies: flurries of trumpets,
beams of waterfalls, transcendent pillows of
     warmth. Upon each resting place I had
made for all my angels, I saw all were good:
     Sleeping, they'd link hands.

RINK AT NORRIE SCHOOL

We never saw the snowplow clearing the new
white away from the center of the baseball field,
but there it was: an unmarked sheet of ice
wrinkled in some places. We stamped our feet
before stepping into the shack and changing
from boots to skates near its fireplace.

Feeling the hot and dry heat of the fireplace
made us more than ready to bear the snow-
flakes already sprinkling and changing
into gentle clumps on our eyelashes. A field
of snowbanks rose all around us as our feet
and ankles wobbled from side to side on the ice:

We had to relearn our balancing acts on the ice.
Skaters around us flew toward the fireplace
at the other end; we began to relax our feet
as we waved bye-bye. Past the banks of snow
we sped and slowed in our circles of the field.
The blade lines on ice underneath kept changing.

We ran and waved at each other, changing
again for the opposite direction. The ice
shrugged at our screams as we crashed into the field
of snowbanked cushions. Smoke from the fireplace
arising above reminded us of the coldness of snow,
but we only wriggled the numb toes of our feet.

We held hands, trying to slide sideways our feet
together like the Olympics on TV without changing
our speed. The ice's unevenness hidden by snow
sometimes tripped us. Getting up from the ice,
we rubbed our sore buttocks before the fireplace
warmed us for a bit. But back onto the field

we jut-tut-tutted before spinning on; the field
of ice swirled with young skaters and fathers on feet.
The eye-jarring cold winds after the fireplace
goaded us on to breakneck speeds, not even changing
as we lifted one foot over another on the ice.
We were trying figure-eights when it began to snow

harder with night. The half-lit field was changing:
More of us wobbled our feet toward the fireplace.
We slid home on icy streets through its powdery snow.

A YOUNG SOLDIER

My weight carried forward by fierce gusts
of icy bullets, I burned sweat flakes
inside my itchy scarf as I swung hands
like pendulums toward the cave-ins. The white
filled with few oases of barren trees
made the distance blinding in my eyes.
I placed my camel's foot slowly after another,
feeling for the hardened snowmobile trails
underneath drifts of this Sahara.
Powders of Rommel's fury melted into drips
from my runny nose. I forced open
my wet eyelashes nearly welded together,
it would've been so easy to drop dead
like Mata Hari who'd learned enough
secrets to last a desert's eternity
and just fall asleep, but oh no, I didn't.
I trudged on to where the deep pool of water
had fluctuated all summer like mercury
inside a thermometer. I clutched broken weeds
sticking out as I wriggled my butt,
yard by yard, toward the water.
Suddenly the ice became too hard under-
neath, I fell into a cascade
not stopping until my feet landed
against the yawning lips of the water.
It gave a weary crack, but the ice was
covered with a foot of snow. I had
no way of knowing how thick the ice was.
I climbed up under the sky's
renewed assault of needles
as my burnt nose dripped like blood.
Among the birches at the edge, I lapsed
into a nap.

Cold kisses awakening
my blinking blind eyes, I found
the world buried in a whiter peace.

AT COPPER PEAK

It was so steep it made us spin
like our plastic toboggans slipping far behind.
    Feelings of dizziness almost did us in.

We were always lucky to find our hats within
climbing distance. It wasn't just an incline,
    it was so steep it made us spin!

From the bottom we barely saw the tin
glare of America's tallest ski jump. Our minds—
    feelings of dizziness—almost did us in.

We punctured with our toes that icy skin
while the sky and sun stayed brilliant as wine.
    It was so steep it made us spin

in circles and wild flops. Like penguins
we waddled, trying to stand up with our sore behinds.
    Feelings of dizziness almost did us in.

We climbed again, higher up in that thin
air, and looked down. Mom's size blew our minds.
    It was so steep it made us spin,
        feelings of dizziness almost did us in.

SWIMMING LESSONS

Dive headfirst from the craggy mountain
of a snowbank into the eye-hurting sea.
Night has unleashed behind a loose foam.

Close your eyes and inhale the icy crystals
melting inside you. Pedal your arms deeper
into the stilled sea of fresh white puffy.

Feel your nose turn beet cold as you exhale
a gasp of icicle clarity. Your eyelids lull easily
with fragments of strange dreams floating.

Calm your neck as the waves above surge,
trickling the gaps in your scarf, mitts, boots.
Dreams drift and sigh without paddling.

ICICLES
for our mother

They have been dripping
for a long time. Outside your bedroom
window. Holding a pane of Norrie Landing.
A fragment of where you are living.

You imagine hearing
the pliths. Of these drops hitting the snow.
These worn-out fox trenches under the eaves.
Under where summer rain runs on gravel.

They have been melting
for a long time. Now.
Only night will heal this bleeding.
But the scab opens easily in the noon sun.

You imagine feeling
the pulse. Of these dropping daggers
finally stabbing the crisp trenches.
With that crunch of ice on ice.

UNDER A NEW MOON

The world outside shone a twilight blue:
Diamonds sprinkled and wrinkled glints
across the night's new dunes of white.
It wrapped us in a mysterious silence
while an occasional car's bright red
devil eyes blinked at the corner
before crawling up Oak Street's incline
past our calmed house. The thermometer
outside our porch window dropped to
a point below zero: We saw its bare
red under the ski caps of snow
and the shaky whiskers of icicles.
Its blood shivered whenever we peered
closer to the cold pane to make sure
it did say what we thought it said.
The solitary porch light shielded us from
the hushed darknesses across the street
and the naked trees unlit by pale warmth.
The dry desert winds tossed flakes
into our faces as we treaded on
the egg's shell of yesterday's snow.
We felt and heard our crunches of boots
as we lifted and placed one foot
ahead of another onto the hard shell.
The snow cracked under the pressure.
Feathery flakes underneath coughed up
and flurried off with the next gust.
We thought of our goose-feathered pillows
where we plucked all night sometimes,
awakening with a curly feather in our noses.
We squinted our eyes as we trooped
past the tired apple tree in our backyard.
Dad's gray picnic table was gone,
folded up and tucked into the back

of our brand-new three-stall garage.
We yelled to each other, *Let's have
a picnic right here!* We thought of
cups of hot chocolate with icebergs
of marshmallows floating to our lips.
Our noses kept dripping even if
we wiped them clean with our mittens,
our eyes were running dry in the moon,
our fingers were beginning to freeze.
We followed each other single file
into the sidedoor, into the hallway,
down to the basement, and took our hats
and boots and mittens and scarves
off to dry near the groaning furnace.
Our ears burned as if on fire.
We ran fingers through our awry hair,
and watched our bangs fly like hands
waving in the hallway mirror. We touched
each other's elbows for that jolt
of static electricity making us bolt.
We wriggled and leaned our numbed toes
against the white kitchen floor
until we could feel the reassurances
of that warm blood returning to
our fingers reaching out for our cups
of hot chocolate and marshmallows.

SPRING

ACORNS II

They fidget when they hear
the murmurs of grasses
stretching their arms to the sky
after a long winter dream of green.
They know it is time,
swelling with restlessness.
They hold their lungs,
filled with a static balloon
of cobweb cold, sighs of patience.
They explode from sheer angst
their blurry-eyed seeds,
telling them to go, go!
They die, listening to
cries of their seeds furrowing
deeper into the warming soil.
Their casket shells are soon
covered by the crowing grass.

IN THE CEMETERY

Next to Montreal River, a land of tombstones
arose from continents of clean snow.
Fog had drifted off, leaving its cool breeze
to brush our necks with a gentle ease.
We stepped around, gingerly. How could we know
precisely where their bodies lay? Oh,
the mystery of paying our respects: Should we bow
our heads and pray . . . ? We shared the unease
next to Montreal River.

Mud emitted belches while virgin grasses glowed
under our boots. Mom and Dad looked at rows
of urns to see if they knew the deceased.
We took to wandering around—no longer acquiesced—
and pointed out funny names, laughs a piece.
Then Dad honked. It was now time to go
across Montreal River.

THE PUDDLE

It was wider than Montreal River,
dark as watered-down brown gravy,
and slow with slags of ice
the color of Fudgesicles.
The great April muck underneath
suckled at my rubber boots
and splashed enough at my folded-in
pants a cold wet with a brown taint.
And who knew how deep it really was
from tracks of spinning tires?
The puddle could consume my entire body
without a burp. I scanned
its expanse as I balanced myself
on its shores of mushy grass.
I climbed the snowbanks, imagined myself
scaling the Himalayas. I'd sight Bigfoot
just as he turned to see me,
his black fur eyebrowed from constant
whirlwinds of snow. He'd flee,
his footprints not surprising me at all.
In that blizzard I'd remain calm,
and he'd return to check me out.
I'd offer a thermos of hot chocolate.
He'd hesitate, but he'd come closer,
his shadow swallowing me
larger than life. His onyx eyes shone
with a bearish warmth as he lifted me
into his arms and swung across
the puddle, the fields, the streets
to downtown where I'd tell the *Daily Globe*.
There was no better shortcut.

SLUSH

O you wondrous gray ooze! We had to run
out in our rubbers and leap high enough
with feet together to make you *SPL-ATT!*
Huge glops of wet exploded everywhere:
You flupped easily car doors, garbage cans,
and mailboxes. We were always careful,
tiptoeing right before your putrid mounds,
and then *Eee-AIK!*
                    That mad jump into grush:
Look how far you'd fly from under our feet!
We outdid Wile E. Coyote in search
of more hills to detonate. We stood there,
enthralled by the ground zero blackness
underneath. And you had splintered into
delicious clumps, thickening slabs ahead.

KNOCKOUT ROUND

tiny tulip fists

boxing a mean left

against the heavyweight snow

toward the first glory of balm

untying and flinging aside

their satin gloves

for a round of applause

in sweaty color.

AT GRANDMA'S HOUSE

Tumbling out of the station wagon, we ran
first around the weeping willow tree
standing guard on the corner of Greenbush
and Coolidge. We giggled when its bead curtains
of tiny reedy leaves flapped with the wind,
exposing our hands clamping on giggles
to Dad waving wildly, beckoning us again
into her house where her molasses
cookies from the oven and milk awaited us.
The soil did not resist our tenners;
it bent with each dent as we waited
for something new to happen: A car
coasting down Greenbush Street to the highway,
or one of us jumping to cartwheel out
into the yielding sun. We kicked at sand
still left over from snowbanks
now peppered islands over the curb, and saw
yellow-green sprouts of grass yawning;
we woke up quite a few baby dandelions too.
Under the sun's eye, we tumbled out
for flight again, this time up the steps
into her warm kitchen where she stood,
looking out her window for each one of us.

SHARDS

The blue egg blotted the green.
I came close to pick and clean.

The pale blue shell was crumpled
into tiny bits, crowded

out by thin clusters of grass.
I tiptoed as if on glass

and squinted up the oak tree.
There wasn't a nest to see.

Right past my eyes flew a red:
I watched the robin head

up to the sky, its wings hard
against the far bluer shard.

THE CEMENT FLOOR

Far left across the street
it lay cracked, a skull of years
behind when it shored up
walls and lockers for miners
showering off rusty dust
from the deep guts of earth,
dark and rusted from ore
powdery from cold boots.

Leftover bricks made pastel
from summer rains dried
into broken pieces of chalk.
We drew hopscotch squares
and built shaky walls, low
houses with rusty tin roofs.
Nights teenagers kicked
them all down in fits of beer.

Each snowflake melting
lopsided each crack, opening
its earthy scalp to worms
furrowing and seeds splitting
into grassy hair gone amok.
It lay there, an earthquake
of wrathful winters felled
by the warmed bricks, inviting.

CATTAILS

East on the railroad tracks   where Dad had brought Daisy
his last cow out to graze   (our house used to be a farm)

A stagnant pond now stands   weary with stilted reeds
their rich brown velvet heads   swollen with the need

To be caressed   bob against each other
the winds tumbleweed   as baby dragonflies scurry

Around the needle pricks   quavering dangerously
above bags of frog eggs   their one gray pupils eyeing

Quick shadows of fat swords   rubbing stabs in the side
long leaves tapering off   its broken tips dunked

When the windows died at night   their last breaths
filled them with enough angst   to lean on each other

SPIDERS
for Eleanor Fraites (in memoriam)

No danger signs prepare you: They drop
like bricks frozen in mid-air in unswept arcades.
You squint for their silken skeletons
by which their lives weave and hang.

Their blueprints nail stupid flies, easily
conned into impotent wrecking balls.
Sunlight strips their musty machinery naked,
constructed sites erected and abandoned.

Leaping off a scaffolding for the next is nothing:
Nimble muscles reel in their oops.
Catch yourself caught unawares by them,
hardhats bred for a life on the run. It's spring.

THE CATERPILLAR QUEEN

Her fuzzy hump, stringed like lapis lazuli
eyes, smoothed from her face as she arched upwards the
branch. When she paused, I blew some breaths at her face.
        Her small incisors
stopped in mid-air but then, she continued her
slinkiness. Her black legs were velvet slippers.
(After all the tree was still young: She'd made a
        list in her mind which
leaves she'd consume gracefully. Oh, she couldn't
wait for that day when she got fat off those boys,
hiding then in her own cocoon, and fling off
        that ugly outfit
days later. Yes, she'd live grandly with her wings!)

Up near where she stopped, many leaves had been chewed
to the bone. They shook nakedly, already
        forsaken in her
presence. I shook her branch. She held on, her thin
slippers now tenacious. Her body flat
against bark, she glared patiently at my hand.
        I bent the branch down,
and let go. She shot into the sky, where she'd
thought she'd soon fly. She writhed on her back in the
grass, her slippers dripping with venom. With a
        leaf from the tree, I
covered her before I squashed her with my foot.
        Her lovesworn boys wept.

APPLE BLOSSOMS

When they appeared, I knew Mom
in her pastel-green hat would hang
loads of white
underwear and training bras
and Dad's undershirts
on the swinging clothesline.

The branches waved hands,
its fragrances rushing to slap
high fives
with the wet clean of our clothes
in the morning shade.
Bees hopped from one branch to another.

I wondered if one of them would fall
off a nervous blossom
into a cranny of my underwear.
But of course: They have wings,
I have eyes,
and we both have noses.

SUMMER

ACORNS III

Drilling fragile roots deeper
into the core of the earth
is a tricky thing. Their translucent
eyes can see only a millimeter
ahead. And when they try
to weave around Old Man Oak's roots,
they find his thickness unassailable.
They slink backwards up, a little,
toward a patch of sunlight.
They know they do not have much
longer to live. When they feel
sun and dew on their bodies,
Old Man Oak hugs them closer
into graveyards of the nameless
around his trunk. He remembers.

A JUNE WEEDING

The sun was still cool.
Tomato leaves heavy with dew
sprinkled giggles on my legs
as I waded through our garden.

I placed Mom's knee pad in an aisle
and watched where my feet rested.
A gush of loam flooded
the warm spaces between my toes.

Kneeling, I arched closer to the leaves
of green beans. Past islands
of shade flickering with my hand,
I caught the furtiveness of a weed.

I felt for its thickest part,
pushing my fingers into the earth.
Its stem was clean with crime.
I tugged slowly and out it came,

white roots gangly with clumps.
It shivered in my hand as
the earth opened an eyelid at me,
surprised. The sun was still cool.

AMONG CLOVERS

Almost noon, the empty baseball field was
strewn with clovers drooping with bees.
Their wings were tiny smokes in the air
as I waved fleshy flies out of my hair
and continued hunting for a four-leaf
clover. My sister Mary had believed
they would bring good luck. On my knees
I looked at each one: too many threes.
My toes curled into the cool blades
underneath as I looked, slowly, this way
and that . . . Oh, there it was! I fell
flat on my stomach, feeling almost unwell
from the sudden movement, the discovery.
I placed my palm behind it: four, not three!
I wanted to shout. The sun hissed on my neck
while sweat made my T-shirt a clinging wreck.
But I felt a sharp itch under my big toe.
I flicked my left foot up in the air,
and laid on my back for a good stare:
A black sliver was studded in the softest part.
How it gleamed like the Tin Man's new heart.
I tweezed it out with the edges of my nails
and tried not to let out gasps or a wail
of pain. I looked for the culprit,
and saw his broken wings couldn't flit.
I flung the sting at him, but he didn't move.
I came closer to look at his black hooves,
struggling to hurry off. I took my four-leaf clover
as I swelled in thongs home. My search was over.

TWO BEARS

Roll up the windows tight now,
Dad said one Sunday afternoon.
The heat inside our station wagon stagnated
as he drove cautiously past
the yellow gateposts into the dump.
We felt almost dizzy from the stench
and pointed out the discarded
junk we could have.
Mom shook her head no every time.

We were halfway through
when Dad stopped. Two black bears
were clawing open
bags for scraps of food.
We tried to keep shushed
as they banged aside
Spam and Campbell's Soup cans.
Flies flitted everywhere.

Then Mark clapped his hands loudly.
We glared at him and then at *them*
as they stopped and stared at our car.
They swaggered slowly toward us,
Mary screamed, *They're coming for us!*
Dad barked through our clamor, *Quiet*.

Their black masses shifted into focus,
grungy fur clotted with dried mud and burs.
Their shiny noses were as big as my fist.
They walked circles around us,
eyeing us. We were a devastated
quiet. I thought of their paws swiping us
down, claws mutilating our bodies.

Suddenly Joe pressed the horn.
We jolted from the sharp bleat.
Carole bellowed hotly, *For gripe's sakes!*

The bears vanished around mountains of bags.
Dad shrugged as he turned the key
and drove us to Hurley
for some ice cream cones at Dairy Queen.
It felt so good
to roll the windows down.

LITTLE GIRL'S POINT

The red cliffs were lined with mud.
It slaked off in huge teardrop sloughs,
a blanket of soppy suctions and plods.
When Dad said it was time to go
home, we planted our toes
and felt the nip of an odd twig.
Each step up made us slide below
where we'd just rigged.

We sought firmer holds of wood,
clapping our hands to make gulls let go
of their perches. Their flood
of wings settled for solitude below.
We had halfway now to go.
It was muddier, too, so we had to dig
faster. It was no longer a show
where we'd just rigged.

Glops of mud whirled around us in floods
as we toiled harder not to slow
down. The Navajo-red mud
made our sun-burned legs and arms glow.
We anchored into the moist cracks so
to suck us in as we tried to dig
the next step up. Then we let go
where we'd just rigged.

The cliffs at last let us go
above to the land of stones, twigs,
and pine cones. We stared below
where we'd just rigged.

THE ANT

He crawled out of his sandy hole
between sidewalks, a trickle of lava
from a volcano. His mind detoured not
when he felt a degree's difference
between the sun and my shadow.
He skirted around for another warm
bite of last night's watermelon.
I trapped him anyway into my circle,
a Mason jar ring. He zigzagged
from one end to another, frantic
with desire to contribute
to the cities humming underground. I held
my head away from my magnifying glass
and aimed my laser ray at him.
He skittered furiously away and around
but I matched his every movement
with my glass. He thrashed with rage,
his blacknesses now a wisp of smoke.
His antennae stopped twitching at last.
I held my hand over him and waited
for my eyes to adjust to the shadow
hanging over him. He was now
an ashy crumb. Death had never seemed
so simple or easy, or so fine.

NEAR BLACK RIVER HARBOR

In the eyes of eyes drinking in sights,
as one might with delicate spirits,
the floor of the huge forestside is a procession.
It is a mere canopy for the Mushroom Lady.

See how she stands her little land:
Once a tiny spore, she has blossomed
into a flaming figure sharply
against the dark colors of the ballroom.

The few lilies of the valley ring chimes.
In a land of the trampled,
she sports a wide-brimmed orange hat
powdered with white freckles.

The weight of fashion bears on her head.
She gets cramps sometimes
in her neck. But it is all right.
She is after all a lady.

THE ABANDONED CAR

Lost since the 1950s, it sat next to the shack
on Taylor and Oak Streets. Its broken headlights
wagged tongues in the wind, its fat lips spreckled
with bird droppings and its painted skin
pockmarked with rust. Andra and I
sneaked quickly as snakes behind the foliage
up along Oak Street, watching the skies
fit black sheets under gray pillows.
Heads bent low, we tiptoed around the car.
Its curves held baskets of dead pine needles.
Up close the car reeked of old Pabst beer cans
and stiffened rags of oil and grease.

We wrapped our hands through the handle, pulling
it down. The door would not budge in our tug-of-war.
We stared at the handle, and suddenly, Andra kicked
the door. It gave a creak, and we pounced on it.
It gave way to the overpowering smell of beer.
Flies were lazy everywhere. I thought of swatting
just so their blood would spurt on the stains
all over the faded turquoise covering. The springs
had already punctured its weary tautness. They
were also covered with rust, tiny flakes of rain
trapped into permanency. We climbed onto the driver's seat,
eyes glued on our bare knees and hands. No more scabs.

Heat sagged inside the car. We could not breathe
in that singeing the back of our legs and elbows.
The flies buzzed slowly but soon settled.
We fiddled with the white knobs on the dashboard.
Nothing happened. We looked at each other,
and began our driving trip. Andra bobbed her head
high as she could above the dashboard. She twisted
the sticky steering wheel back and forth: We drove

downtown past Lopez's IGA Store, past the drive-in theater.
We stayed on the U.S. Highway 2 to nowhere
back to Oak and Taylor. Then we saw
Mr. Talasky wave amiably to his black dogs.

We ducked beneath the dashboard
while I stared at her eyes darting around,
her finger poised on her lips.
A terse minute passed before she craned
her head above. My neck was stiff from
all that holding, trying not to choke from
the mustiness all around. We peered around
and ducked again when we felt a thunderclap
rumble through the car. We kicked at
the door with our feet, banging it open.

Down the cracked sidewalks past three more houses
we ran, slipped into the dry cocoon of our sidedoor.
We wiped the plump raindrops off our sticky arms.
The kitchen window was painted with rain.
The angry skies at last spent, the sun cast
a metallic glow on everything,
like the car we drove in our dreams.

THE DEAD SKUNK

Joe, you found it that July
near the edges of the cave-ins.
You dared to poke it
with a stick, and found its brown eyes glassy.
You ran home with Paul and Randy
and took a rope from the red garage.
You tied it to its tail and dragged it
over the small hills and around saplings.
It was so fat it flip-
flopped from one side to another
across Oak Street. You climbed
up the gray telephone pole
in front of our house. I came out
and watched you fling the rope
over a hook. You jumped down
and pulled it so the skunk swung
upside-down, and back and forth.
Its belly quivered from bouncing off the pole.
Then we saw Father Frank coming up the street
on his daily afternoon walk. You waved
and said, *Good afternoon*. He nodded
but said nothing. He moved quickly
on up the street while we held in our guffaws.
It now hung still, and you said
we all could take turns pulling the rope.
Finally. My turn: I felt its weight
slip in my hands, I couldn't believe
how heavy it was, I almost lost the rope.
But I tugged it firmly and watched the skunk
sway. You grinned as I held on to
the rope for its dear life.

WILD STRAWBERRIES

They were covered with fitted hangnails,
green and small as my fingernails;
their vines crept rollercoasters through
thatches of grass. I knew
they'd wake up one morning without fail,
suddenly embarrassed about being so pale.
That was when they allowed that detail
of turning red instead of some autumn hue.
So they were covered,
a sweet August happily veiled.

I watched for them when I walked the trails
across the street at noon.
They blended in with their grasses' hues
easily; I found them sometimes under my shoes.
But when they glowed rubies by the trails,
they were uncovered.

A BURIAL

The beetle's black back was smooth as pistachios;
his antennae stood like strands of string. The Jif jar
had been his home for six days when he died. (Lettuce
stolen from our garden had sustained him
through.) The glass once fogged with his breaths
was now clear. I stared at his stilled body,

leaning it sideways against the glass. His body
slid and bounced, almost like pistachios,
as I carried him; I kept my breaths
away from the lid's nail holes of the jar.
But before I could dig and bury him,
I had to pluck some fresh lettuce.

(Underground, he would need lettuce
to survive; after all, nobody
down there could possibly care for him
as much as I did. He couldn't eat pistachios,
or hard foods; what else could I put in his jar?)
Somberness pervaded each one of my breaths.

I twisted open the jar for his final breaths
before I slipped a Ziploc bag over the lettuce
and his body under the lid. (The jar
was perfect, filled with food just for somebody
like him. There were no stones like pistachios:
Everything had been chosen green and tender for him.)

As I began digging, I kept an eye on him.
The shade of the house next door eased my breaths
as I made a pile of dirt next to where pistachio
shells were strewn by the red garage. Lettuce
glistened, curtains inside a casket body,
in the concave security of the jar.

The hole was now big enough for the jar.
I mouthed a Hail Mary as I looked at him
one last time. I shook his body,
a little, to where he could breath
in more of all that sweet lettuce.
Soil fell on his lid like pistachios.

I imagined his jar misted with sweet breaths
as his pistachio back leaned against the lettuce.
There would be nobody quite like him.

DARKLY WENT THE WIND

Chariots of death-blue clouds roared
as I kicked off my thongs. I spun
my arms like a trapeze artist tumbling,
scaling mountain after mountain
shrinking a dark green in that calm.

The distance of trees turned the color
of a black slate just washed clean.
My feet felt again the coolness of soil
seeping, and again, as I ran and leaped
as if the earth was my trampoline.

The skies soon became a circus tent.
Darkly went the wind after me,
warning me madly higher and higher
until I was the height of each gust.
Then the first whip of rain cracked.

AUTUMN

ACORNS IV

They've just had the finest party,
jingling in the wind and tittering
from each shame-on-you scold
from Old Man Oak. They plead
for constant forgiveness,
another day and night more.
But he becomes oh so moody, harsh.
They grumble, Why? You're no fun
anymore. We don't like the cold.
They feel themselves turning tired,
hardly young now. They look
sideways at each other,
not believing they could go anytime.
They close their eyes when they hear
one of them fall off a branch.
They look down, and shake their heads,
knowing they too must dig
their own graves back home.

THE TREE

It stood in one corner of our backyard,
littering the grass with khaki peas
along with twigs and huge bark shards.
We climbed its nailed-on bars with ease.

Littering the grass with khaki peas
stuck between our toes, we inched around
and climbed its nailed-on bars with ease.
Once up we heard Dad yelling, *Down!*

Stuck up there on toes, we inched around
branches and watched the world below:
Once up, we heard Dad yelling, *Down!*
The sunset gave our squints a glow.

Branches: We watched the world below.
Mr. Lewinski plucked his last weed
as sunsets gave our squints a glow.
The cool breezes made us feel free

as Mr. Lewinski plucked his last weed.
We pretended to be planes or Peter Pan,
the cool breezes made us feel free.
We knew there were other unknown lands:

We pretended to be planes or Peter Pan.
Step by step we hugged downwards the tree;
we knew there were other unknown lands
of games. We stood around, waiting,

step by step. We hugged downwards the tree
in finding Dad and two men with a chainsaw.
Of games, we stood around waiting:
They seemed indifferent to our sense of awe

in finding Dad and two men with a chainsaw.
The noise was so loud we covered our ears.
They seemed indifferent to our sense of awe
at chips flying off in resinous tears,

the noise was that loud. We covered our ears
as it tottered to a thundering crash
at chips flying off in resinous tears.
The trunk was marked off for cash.

As it tottered to a thundering crash,
we wondered how long it'd take to grow back.
The trunk was marked off for cash:
We watched them aim their axes to hack.

We wondered how long it'd take to grow back
along with twigs and huge bark shards.
We watched them aim their axes to hack
as the tree fell apart in our backyard.

FIREFLIES

for John Lee Clark

Sunsets strike their match. Aflame,
they awaken to flee their day cage.

Master of their own illusions,
they perform tricks onstage.

Night after night, they surprise
flickering lights out of thin air.

They are a Morse code of blips,
too quick to decode. We stare.

We chase them with our jars,
open with lids of punched holes.

They dart away. We stand
watching the autumn of our souls.

SUNFLOWER SEEDS

That September the sunflowers rose to a tottering height.
The yellow petals were tired from the buffeting winds;
their faces had bunched up, its muscles heavy with seed
and sore from birdbeaks pecking for just one more.
Their stalks were thick as joints. The caw-caws
of crows reverberated from the Walquists's backyard tree

between our garden and theirs. They swooped from the tree
when no one was around, and scaled back the heights
with seeds in their beaks. We knew from their caws
they had succeeded again, with the winds
carrying them higher to their perches once more.
I checked the soil below the sunflowers for fallen seeds,

and rubbed them clean. I popped one of the seeds
into my mouth, and felt its sharp edges. The tree's
shade had already darkened in the evening sun a bit more
while the crows shifted their claws in their heights.
I turned my face toward the wind
and closed my eyes. Instead I heard their caw-caws.

I looked up and saw sparrows swooping low. Caw-caw?
Did I truly hear something? I chewed on another seed
as I watched dandelion whiskers tossing in the wind
and then a chipmunk skittering up the tree.
I leaned back to look at the sunflower faces from my height,
and saw seeds. There were still a lot more.

I pulled one stalk down more
to the side until I could pluck its seeds. Caw-caws
thundered in my ears, and I searched the heights
of the tree for them. I cupped my hand to hold my seeds
as I stood back to let the stalk go. The tree's
branches fluttered when loose seeds crossed the wind.

I went to the shed's bench nearby. The wind
carried sparrows to a perfect stop for more
rest. The crows let out a series of caw-caws
as they sailed down, expectantly, from the tree.
I placed on the bench my remaining seeds
and clapped my hands like thunder from the heights.

Away in the wind they carried their caw-caws.
I popped in another seed and eyed the tree
for more dares from their heights.

ONE INDIAN SUMMER

The sun came out and stilled
everything for a moment:
The grasses stopped fading,
the daffodils stopped drooping,
the leaves stopped falling.
It was chilly, even with
a sweatshirt on. I sat outside,
my feet swinging over the edge
of that rusty red wagon,
and closed my eyes.
The sun lathered warmth
all over my face.

The clouds would
stretch or fatten their bodies;
I'd have to guess
what they were before
they changed again.
Sometimes I couldn't wait
and peeked through my hands.
They stopped when they knew
I was watching them undress
into something else.
But I couldn't help it.
They were so voluptuous.

MRS. KICHAK'S PLUM TREE

It never grew large.
Its two-inch thorns cast needles
in winter. No one went near.

But came autumns when we stole
its plums, big as robin's eggs.
We bit into them behind our shack

where bittersweet juices dribbled
out of our mouths' corners.
Crime had never tasted so sweet.

How its embittered bark fell
in angry chips every autumn
all over the soft tufts.

WET LEAVES

Rain dumped its paint bucket
all over the trees on Oak Street.
The walls of autumn had no color
but its chill took forever to dry.
Its odorless fumes sank heavily,
leaving a numbness in our feet.
Everything had a cold blanket.

Trees shivered as its leaves fell,
slapping sidewalks with tears.
They puffed their last breaths,
bleeding onto the broken cement.
When at last the paint dried,
we peeled the leaves, uncovering
a wallpaper of summer souls.

THE FOX

for James Thomas Sharer 1964 - 2007

Near the cave-in's edge, I slithered
through a welt of birches. The sun
knifed a swath for mosquitoes
to pursue my feverish dreams.
As a safari guide somewhere in Africa,
I knew where all the wild cats hid,
crouching in a sleepless repose
amidst the plains that would be mine
had I lived in Kenya. I peered
beyond the birches to observe you.

Scavenging had turned your orangeness
into a brown dullness that darted
among the grasses of beckoning
the winter to come. I stood
still with no rifle to call mine.
You froze, turned, held
your bushy tail high and proud,
tilted your ears in a flick,
then rocketed, a sleek rustle before
the jungle of grass ensnared your prey.

OCTOBER WALK

Loose leaves crackled as I dragged
my tenners through the sidewalk
piles of leaves by the Roths's house.
I felt acorns under my soles
and kicked them far across
sludges of dirty leaves
glued together by rains.

The leaves were a soggy golden
papier-mâché for the brown ones.
They never got carried away
by the sudden winds like the others
around them. They stayed flat,
muck over dying grasses
combed tight against the sidewalk.

The next acorn I kicked leaped
over sidewalk cracks into the shrubs.
A chipmunk stood silent,
his shiny eyes yielding nothing.
My acorn had fallen inches near
him. I matched his silence,
my muscles rigid as his.

His paws held a split acorn.
Had he been eating until I came along?
His throat showed no swallowing
motions. I held my breath,
then he shot up
the trunk. A Buick had sped by,
I looked up, he was gone.

HOW JONAS FOUND HIS WAY HOME

The first twenty years had been hard
for Old Man Oak, hearing the chippies whimper
as cold raindrops drenched his thick bark.
He adored their tiny paws skipping
through his armpits. Such tenderness made up
for the loneliness of winters. Cars turning
the corner of Spruce and Oak Streets
never waited long enough for conversation.

Old Man Oak was young, then,
and in love with their games. He loved the sound
of their giggles, enough to give tremors time
and again just to hear them titter once more.
Even then he could not let go the weight
of all these acorns clinging to his arms.
Why, each one had a nickname and dreams
of their own, filled with growing up
tall and strong and wise as Old Man Oak.

One November forty years ago, he learned.
Jonas, a bookish chippy, loved reading
about life beyond Oak Street in the fine print
of striped grasses and gnarly twigs.
He was known for his habit of pushing up his glasses
to read more. The candy wrappers trapped in nets
of grasses fascinated him for hours, his eyes
sparkling with something startling. He was
convinced that he did not have to scavenge
for winter food. The changes of autumn did
not faze him: He had read human neighbors
would toss out seeds, old apples, anything,
whenever they spied a lonely animal
outside their snow-capped windowsills.

Jonas was hunched behind a tuft
of grass, reading a Zane Grey western
about an oak fledgling's battle to claim
land over a spiteful weed, when Old Man Oak
noticed him. Jonas was far too skinny,
not fattened enough to last the coming winter.
He knew in his roots it would be a harsh one.
One hundred and twenty inches would fall,
and the cold would freeze his digging paws.
Old Man Oak envied Jonas's total absorption,
but no, it was time.

He spoke in a low whisper: *Jonas?*
The chippy didn't look up at all. He turned
over the grass blade, his eyes bulging
at the description of two different roots
braiding around each other, trying to strangle
each other. He even ignored those tremors.
Old Man Oak thought of all those chippies
settling in their nests, loaded with acorns
ripped very painfully, as it were, from his arms.
He wondered how to explain how
books could not substitute life . . .

But then a sparrow swooped right above
Jonas such that his glasses fell off.
He fumbled about blindly, his paws reaching
out into the Technicolor of confusion.
Old Man Oak tried not to laugh at
the sad spectacle; the glasses were
right behind him! But he had other ideas.
He shook an arm, trying not to wince from
the rupture an acorn from his skin;
it was worse than a band-aid. It fell down
on Jonas's head. His nose throbbed and
ached from smelling the sweet nut inside.
He cradled it in his arm, and stepped
cautiously into the treacherous grass.

Old Man Oak shook another acorn off,
nailing him again. As he did so,
he sensed a hundred chippies awakening
to the drip-drop of acorns falling.
How Old Man Oak wept freely
when Jonas blundered and found his glasses,
seeing for the first time and pointing
this way to the acorns.

THE TRESPASSER

One November afternoon I ignored
for the first time those signs
(PRIVATE PROPERTY - DO NOT TRESSPASS)
surrounding their gray faces
shaded by evergreen hues. I leaped
across the steep cleft
to the rusty barbed wires. I watched
my body hold like Baryshnikov
as I transferred parts of my body,
one by one, between the fenceposts,
until I was complete
on the other side. I looked beyond
the motorcycle trails, and felt
different. The woods had been so easy
to find my way through, but now—
I sensed a shaking branch
and caught in time
the beady eyes of a fat squirrel.
His bushy tail vanished into
the grayness of the sky hanging low.
I turned around to see if
anyone could see me from the road.
Satisfied, I took my time clearing
the fragile and prickly curtains of branches
snapping, or slapping back
with a sudden ferocity. I found myself
breathing more slowly, the winds
no longer living here. I was
filled with the color of ashes.
I felt the softness of stillness
bend tenderly under my feet
as I sought a place deep inside there
where no one would see me.
The branches made for hard going.

When I stopped at last, I could see
barely the weak sun filtering through.
I sat down on a rotting log, and
broke off a huge chunk of brown moss.
It crumbled in my hand. I licked
my finger and held it out for
any sign of the wind. Nothing.
I kicked at the gray ground
and watched pink centipedes
flail madly in their cool nightmares.
They crept back into their blankets.
The soil was dark, dark with life.
I zipped up my jacket once more,
and suddenly felt a flutter
of wind, of wings, of wonder.
Dull yellow eyes of a brown owl
peered down at me. His eyes
did not blink, not even once.
His perfect silence terrified me.
As I hurried toward the fence,
I looked back. He only cocked
his pointed ears at me, asking
with those eyes an enormous why.

GOLDENRODS
for our father 1926 - 1989

Summers ago when we used to play hide-and-seek across the street,
its voluptuous boughs ganged up on us,
its gold powder smudging our arms. We ran too fast
sometimes, its stiff leaves scratching our legs;
how good it felt then to stand in a clearing,
where forget-me-nots and lazy-eyed susans led
way to a breeze tickling
our exposed legs. There we stood, rubbing
and waving off the mosquitoes. In time we came to ignore
those yellow things.
There were so many of them.

> *Years have passed; I have forgotten about them*
> *until now. I had never thought of them as*
> *weeds.*

They are still standing in the November winds,
brown-starved for a little more warmth. Their rickety stems are
now hollowed out from the creeping chill. Of course
they have endured all this before—they let fall
their seeds on the moist patches of the earth, sprouting
so many more like them. They stand silent
when dozens of their kind are trampled upon; they huddle together
amidst hailstorms and wreckages. They have
no other protection against their kind. They do not question
why, and never how else should they live. They are too busy
preparing for the next smothering of winter.

> *It occurs to me now they are stronger than we. They have been*
> *expecting all this. How much faith they hold in their own*
> *seeds.*

FINDING MY WAY TO THE ACORNS
An Afterword

This book may have first appeared in 2002, but I'd more or less finished it in the fall of 1990. Technically it's over two decades old, but emotionally it's a lifetime old. In your hands are snapshots from a time no longer mine.

Time is a peculiar creature.

It's hard to pinpoint how a book of poems like this one gets born.

One could say, "Start anywhere, and you'll find a path soon enough."

When my mother sent me a newspaper clipping of Gerard Lauzon's photograph depicting the steeple of my family's church being knocked over back in 1986, I was devastated. It didn't matter that I'd sworn never to attend Mass after I came out as a gay man. My negative experiences as a deaf student in the Ironwood Catholic School system had resulted in a deep distrust of organized religion in general, and the way the Catholic Church had treated LGBT people hadn't helped matters any.

Still, I couldn't believe that anyone would raze the church. *My* church! The landmark had cast a deep shadow over my childhood. It was through the Church that I saw the barely existent line between piety and hypocrisy. I also learned how arrogant and patronizing priests and nuns could be, and I learned to feel guilty and ashamed of being myself. One would think that I'd have been too delighted to see a monument to hypocrisy and meaningless rituals wiped from the face of the earth.

But no. Deep down inside me was the faint glimmer that maybe—just *maybe!*—the Church would finally accept me as one of them and make me feel like one of the family, much like I'd longed to be accepted by my own hearing family. If I wanted to return to the Church, no other church than St. Michael's would do. Even though I've visited a number of architecturally great churches, St. Michael's was the only one that represented the Church, period.

Gerard Lauzon's picture was the catalyst of what became the first of many drafts of *St. Michael's Fall*. (The picture later appeared on its cover when Deaf Life Press published it in 1996.) Back then, though, I was never satisfied with many of its poems, but I couldn't pinpoint why.

In the spring of 1990 I won a scholarship to attend Marilyn Hacker's workshop on traditional forms at the Poetry Society of America. I couldn't believe it. Ms. Hacker had been a literary idol of mine ever since I read her exquisitely written sonnet novel *Love, Death, and the Changing of the Seasons*. It didn't matter that her narrator was an older lesbian in love with a younger woman; each page was fraught with equal doses of drama, love, and ache, rendered carefully in pitch-perfect lines. There was also another reason why I couldn't believe my luck. We had to submit our work for her consideration, so only twelve of us were chosen for the workshop. My poems were good enough to get me in? Wow.

Most participants in writing workshops have a wide variety of experience levels. A few are truly talented with something to say; most were average with a lot of potential; and a few couldn't truly write anything. Not so with Marilyn's workshop. All twelve of us were so good, so good that a few of us made a point of showing up early in a friendly competitive environment to see if we could come up with a great sestina, a knockout sapphic, and so on. Using Philip Dacey and David Jauss's *Strong Measures: Contemporary American Poetry in Traditional Forms* as our text, she assigned us specific forms to try out each week. That anthology, a landmark title in the burgeoning New Formalist movement, literally changed my life as a poet. Suddenly, formal and metrical poetry wasn't for the stiff-lipped lost in the shadows of the ivory tower. There were so many different ways to do a sonnet, a rondeau, and so many other forms that I couldn't stop playing with each one. It was like toying around with one musical instrument after another. I couldn't get enough!

It was through that workshop I'd realized what was wrong with the poems I'd written for *St. Michael's Fall*. There wasn't a *musical* subtext for the story I wanted to tell. Even though the narrative was about a deaf boy growing up deaf and oralist in a small town during the 1970s, it needed an *ear*. It needed tunes of a different sort.

With that revelation alone, I was off and running with my new poems for *St. Michael's Fall*.

By that point I had been living in New York City for almost two years; I'd moved there after graduating from Gallaudet in May 1988. I first lived in the Greenpoint neighborhood of Brooklyn, and moved again a year later to a fifth-floor walkup off the corner of West 4th and West 10th Streets, a block north of Christopher Street and Seventh Avenue South in Greenwich Village. My tiny room had no air conditioning, but I didn't mind that so much. It had two windows that faced each other, and my futon bed sat between them. When the windows were opened, the wind of many smells from nearby apartments swooshed in all over me. I never needed an alarm clock because a neighbor's coffee machine always woke me up.

Everything felt tiny and yet oversized everywhere I looked once I stepped out on West 4th Street. The neighborhood soon felt familiar to me, but I missed the comfort and solitude of the woods across the street from where I'd grown up. There was something about being lost in the trees and the greenery that soothed me. Central Park wasn't enough. As big as it was, it was often overrun with people.

I began remembering.

There is childhood, and then there is childhood.

The first one is the one we grow into. The second one is the one we remember long after our onset of puberty.

Gallaudet University in the fall of 1984 gave me the self-confidence I'd lacked in the first 18 years of my life in hearing schools. For once, on a campus full of deaf students, I wasn't anyone special. I learned ASL quickly, and it wasn't long before I had the courage to be out as a gay man. I cast off the shackles of my wallflowered childhood. I wanted nothing of my old life where I had been made fun of and treated as a second-class citizen.

That was another reason why Gerard Lauzon's photograph had hit me so hard halfway through my college years. I had thought I was finished with my old life.

I tried not to remember, but its shrill notes, echoey like the big organ that Mrs. Pavlovich used to play during Mass at St. Michael's, bypassed my brain right into the ear of my heart. There, each memory was played, and replayed, like a vinyl record with its needle jumping right back to the beginning.

What did it mean to be deaf, and not allowed to use sign language, while filling up with difficult questions about what it meant to be a Catholic?

The summer of 1990 in New York City was a hot one. I couldn't wait to get home from my demanding job at Grey Advertising and resume working on *St. Michael's Fall*. Imperceptibly at first, I began writing about my experiences in the woods across the street from my mother's house. After all, on the other side of the cave-ins stood the proud spire of St. Michael's. It made sense at the time to include those poems as part of *St. Michael's Fall*.

Ronnie Cohen, one of my friends from Marilyn's workshop, and I got together fairly often to discuss poetry and literature. He was a straight hearing student who'd taken a number of creative writing classes at Columbia University. He then lived in Park Slope, and his apartment was a few blocks away from Prospect Park, the "Central Park" of Brooklyn. One Saturday afternoon in August Ronnie and I walked through the park. I chanced upon an acorn by the paved trail and picked it up. In that moment I realized why *St. Michael's Fall* had long felt lugubrious. The nature poems were getting in the way of the book's larger narrative!

Later that evening I took stock of my nature poems and saw to my shock that if I wrote maybe six more nature poems, I could have a brand-new full-length collection separate from *St. Michael's Fall*!

I still have that acorn somewhere in my possession.

Even though the poems in this book never talk about my deafness, they were very much informed by how I navigated the world across the street. I have enough residual hearing to enable the use of powerful hearing aids, but I have terrible sound location skills. When alone, I have to be on the constant lookout for birds swooping low and branches flapping from the gusts above me. And because I couldn't always follow what my eight siblings said around the kitchen table, I fell into the habit of daydreaming what they were *actually* saying.

That led to my habit of imagining what animals and plants were thinking when I was alone in the woods. Even though I wasn't writing much back then, I was already becoming a storyteller.

My father died suddenly of a heart attack on October 26, 1989. By then I had been living in New York for 14 months.

It was a shock. My grandmother's death on October 22, 1977, affected me deeply, but this was very different. Dad? Gone? Impossible.

During that week in my mother's house I was filled with detachment, wondering what was going to happen next. I had to think of my house not as my house, as in Dad and Mom living there, but as my mother's house for the first time.

Snow fell, crowning the forlorn goldenrods across the street. A wind made them shiver. I felt an intense ache, which I couldn't articulate at the time. When I finally did, though, I didn't know what to do with "Goldenrods." If I wanted to use "Montreal River" as the closing poem for *St. Michael's Fall*, I had a problem. Where could "Goldenrods" possibly go?

I put it aside for the time being.

On my way home on the subway after picking up that acorn in Prospect Park, I realized that "Goldenrods" could be the new book's closing poem. I only had to begin with my winter poems and organize the rest by season.

Years later I became friends with John Lee Clark, the editor of *The Tactile Mind*, a quarterly that showcased the creative work of the Deaf and signing communities. He wanted me to submit my work, so we corresponded a bit via email. We finally met in person at a pizzeria on Hennepin Avenue in Minneapolis. We hit it off. I was still living in New York City.

He had liked *St. Michael's Fall*. That was how he'd initially learned of my work. He didn't ask if I had another poetry collection at the time.

Later, when he decided to go into publishing books, he asked me if I had anything for his consideration. I couldn't believe it when he accepted *This Way to the Acorns*. He proved to be a tough editor, but in a good way. I understood he wanted the book to be a solid collection, so throughout the spring of 2002, John tightened the longer poems while I rewrote the old poems and created new poems. "Fireflies" and "The Fox" came up as a result of John requesting that each seasonal section have only twelve poems each. The autumn section had needed two more to round out the book.

If *St. Michael's Fall* had been a snapshot of me trying to master my craft as a young poet, *This Way to the Acorns* was a snapshot of me finding surer footing. I had become a better photographer.

When I rewrite a poem, I often aim for a beginning, a middle, and an ending of sorts. Those three components may not always be in chronological order, but all three must be there, somewhere in the poem itself, to achieve a sense of motion and emotion. I also find that when I perform such poems onstage, they work really well for audiences. Everyone likes stories, so if I can reduce their initial resistance to poetry through the guise of storytelling, why, all the better!

Because this book was about childhood, it made sense to incorporate a sense of stories growing like strawberry vines everywhere.

The summer of 1990 was my first important awakening as a writer. I was literally exploding daily with new poems, short stories, and essays: *St. Michael's Fall*, *Mute*, and *This Way to the Acorns*, as well as my national breakthrough *Christopher Street* piece "Notes of a Deaf Gay Writer" and huge chunks of *Men with Their Hands*, were written in the same five-month period.

But out of all that inspired frenzy I remember most the overwhelming feelings of tenderness and loss for the child I used to be in the woods across the street, and for the father I'd lost. That's why *This Way to the Acorns* often strikes me as a scrapbook.

Poets and philosophers in their work have long expounded on memory and its vestiges.

When I write, it's not just because I want to communicate. I also want to remember. No, no—that's not quite correct either. I want to leave behind something that others can remember long after I'm gone. I would expect that sometime in the future, books about what nature was like before so much of it disappeared in global warming will become quite precious.

We will long for nature in the same way we already long for low gas prices. Back then we didn't need to think much of taking road trips just about anywhere, or the cumulatively negative effects our driving could have on the environment.

Some will persist in wanting to know how a book begins. Like each child growing up, each book grows up differently. The paths I took to finish *St. Michael's Fall*, *This Way to the Acorns*, and my other collections couldn't be more different from each other. Which is the way it should be.

Once, after reading this book, a friend said to me: "But each experience you had while growing up across the street from your home was a poem waiting to be remembered."

I think that best sums up my feelings about *This Way to the Acorns*.

Thank you for remembering with me.

ABOUT THE AUTHOR

Raymond Luczak grew up in Ironwood and Houghton, Michigan, in a family of nine children, in which he was number seven and the only one deaf. After graduating from high school, he attended Gallaudet University in Washington, D.C., where he earned a B.A. in English. A few months later he moved to New York City, where he would live for seventeen years. It was there that he began creating the first of his books. Titles include *Assembly Required: Notes from a Deaf Gay Life* (RID Press) and *Men with Their Hands: A Novel* (Queer Mojo), which won first place in the Project: QueerLit 2006 Contest.

In addition to working with the acclaimed storyteller Mario Hernandez for the DVD *Manny ASL: Stories in American Sign Language*, he directed and edited the full-length documentaries *Guy Wonder: Stories & Artwork* and *Nathie: No Hand-Me-Downs*. He is also a playwright with nineteen plays performed in three countries.

In 2005, he relocated to Minneapolis, Minnesota. Sibling Rivalry Press will publish his fifth collection of poems *How to Kill Poetry* in the spring of 2013.

www.raymondluczak.com

www.ingramcontent.com/pod-product-compliance
Lightning Source LLC
La Vergne TN
LVHW091206080426
835509LV00006B/853